How would you like to give this book to all of your stakeholders (clients, employees, partners, etc.)?

We can create a customized copy for you where we:
1) Put a reference to you on the front and back covers, or make you the co-author, and
2) Put a letter from you that replaces this page.

We can't imagine a better way for you to say Thank You! Can you?

Thank You!

Saying "Thank You!" in 140 Languages

Mitchell Levy

E-mail: info@thinkaha.com
20660 Stevens Creek Blvd., Suite 210
Cupertino, CA 95014

Published by THiNKaha®
20660 Stevens Creek Blvd., Suite 210, Cupertino, CA 95014
http://thinkaha.com
E-mail: info@thinkaha.com

First Printing: March 2017
Paperback ISBN: 978-1-61699-209-5 (1-61699-209-3)
eBook ISBN: 978-1-61699-210-1 (1-61699-210-7)
Place of Publication: Silicon Valley, California, USA
Paperback Library of Congress Number: 2017901911

Trademarks

All terms mentioned in this book that are known to be trademarks or service marks have been appropriately capitalized. Neither THiNKaha, nor any of its imprints, can attest to the accuracy of this information. Use of a term in this book should not be regarded as affecting the validity of any trademark or service mark.

Warning and Disclaimer

Every effort has been made to make this book as complete and as accurate as possible. The information provided is on an "as is" basis. The author(s), publisher, and their agents assume no responsibility for errors or omissions. Nor do they assume liability or responsibility to any person or entity with respect to any loss or damages arising from the use of information contained herein.

The phrase "Thank You!" is a way of
expressing our gratitude. When a person has
done us a favor and we want to express our
feelings of gratitude for the deed, it is one of
the times when we would use the phrase.

1

140 languages to say "Thank You!"
http://aha.pub/thankyou

_____

_____

_____

2

Thank you! (in English) – in 140 languages
http://aha.pub/thankyou

_____

_____

_____

3

Dankie! (Thank You! in Afrikaans) –
in 140 languages http://aha.pub/thankyou

_____

_____

_____

4

Faleminderit! (Thank You! in Albanian) –
in 140 languages http://aha.pub/thankyou

_____

_____

_____

5

Eskerrik asko! (Thank You! in Basque) –
in 140 languages http://aha.pub/thankyou

_____

_____

_____

6

Hvala ti! (Thank You! in Bosnian) –
in 140 languages http://aha.pub/thankyou

_____

_____

_____

7

Gràcies! (Thank You! in Catalan) – in 140 languages http://aha.pub/thankyou

_____

_____

_____

8

Salamat! (Thank You! in Cebuano) – in 140 languages http://aha.pub/thankyou

_____

_____

_____

9

Xièxiè! (Thank You! in Chinese) –
in 140 languages http://aha.pub/thankyou

_____

_____

_____

10

Grazie! (Thank You! in Corsican) –
in 140 languages http://aha.pub/thankyou

_____

_____

_____

11

Hvala ti! (Thank You! in Croatian) –
in 140 languages http://aha.pub/thankyou

_____

_____

_____

12

Děkuji! (Thank You! in Czech) –
in 140 languages http://aha.pub/thankyou

_____

_____

_____

13

tak! (Thank You! in Danish) –
in 140 languages http://aha.pub/thankyou

_____

_____

_____

14

Dank je! (Thank You! in Dutch) –
in 140 languages http://aha.pub/thankyou

_____

_____

_____

15

Dankon! (Thank You! in Esperanto) –
in 140 languages http://aha.pub/thankyou

_____

_____

_____

16

Aitäh! (Thank You! in Estonian) – in 140 languages http://aha.pub/thankyou

_____

_____

_____

17

Salamat! (Thank You! in Filipino) – in 140 languages http://aha.pub/thankyou

_____

_____

_____

18

Kiitos! (Thank You! in Finnish) –
in 140 languages http://aha.pub/thankyou

_____

_____

_____

19

Je vous remercie! (Thank You! in French) –
in 140 languages http://aha.pub/thankyou

_____

_____

_____

20

Grazas! (Thank You! in Galician) –
in 140 languages http://aha.pub/thankyou

_____

_____

_____

21

გმადლობთ! (Thank You! in Georgian) –
in 140 languages http://aha.pub/thankyou

_____

_____

_____

22

አመሰግናለሁ! (Thank You! in Amharic) –
in 140 languages http://aha.pub/thankyou

_____

_____

_____

23

ՇՆՈՐՀԱԿԱԼՈՒԹՅՈՒՆ! (Thank You! in Armenian)
– in 140 languages http://aha.pub/thankyou

_____

_____

_____

24

Təşəkkür edirəm! (Thank You!
in Azerbaijani) – in 140 languages
http://aha.pub/thankyou

_____

_____

_____

25

Дзякуй! (Thank You! in Belarusian) –
in 140 languages http://aha.pub/thankyou

_____

_____

_____

26

ধন্যবাদ! (Thank You! in Bengali) –
in 140 languages http://aha.pub/thankyou

27

Благодаря! (Thank You! in Bulgarian) –
in 140 languages http://aha.pub/thankyou

28

Vielen Dank! (Thank You! in German) –
in 140 languages http://aha.pub/thankyou

_____

_____

_____

29

Ευχαριστώ! (Thank You! in Greek) –
in 140 languages http://aha.pub/thankyou

_____

_____

_____

30

આભાર! (Thank You! in Gujarati) –
in 140 languages http://aha.pub/thankyou

_____

_____

_____

31

Mèsi! (Thank You! in Haitian) –
in 140 languages http://aha.pub/thankyou

_____

_____

_____

32

na gode! (Thank You! in Hausa) –
in 140 languages http://aha.pub/thankyou

_____

_____

_____

33

Mahalo! (Thank You! in Hawaiian) –
in 140 languages http://aha.pub/thankyou

_____

_____

_____

34

धन्यवाद! (Thank You! in Hindi) -
in 140 languages http://aha.pub/thankyou

_____

_____

_____

35

Ua tsaug rau koj! (Thank You! in Hmong) -
in 140 languages http://aha.pub/thankyou

_____

_____

_____

36

Köszönöm! (Thank You! in Hungarian) –
in 140 languages http://aha.pub/thankyou

_____

_____

_____

37

Þakka þér! (Thank You! in Icelandic) –
in 140 languages http://aha.pub/thankyou

_____

_____

_____

38

Daalụ! (Thank You! in Igbo) –
in 140 languages http://aha.pub/thankyou

_____

_____

_____

39

Terima kasih! (Thank You! in Indonesian) – in 140 languages http://aha.pub/thankyou

_____

_____

_____

40

Go raibh maith agat! (Thank You! in Irish) –
in 140 languages http://aha.pub/thankyou

_____

_____

_____

41

Grazie! (Thank You! in Italian) –
in 140 languages http://aha.pub/thankyou

42

Arigatōgozaimashita! (Thank You!
in Japanese) – in 140 languages
http://aha.pub/thankyou

43

Matur nuwun! (Thank You! in Javanese) –
in 140 languages http://aha.pub/thankyou

_____

_____

_____

44

ಧನ್ಯವಾದಗಳು! (Thank You!
in Kannada) – in 140 languages
http://aha.pub/thankyou

_____

_____

_____

45

Рақмет сізге (Thank You! in Kazakh) – in 140 languages http://aha.pub/thankyou

_____

_____

_____

46

អរគុណ! (Thank You! in Khmer) –
in 140 languages http://aha.pub/thankyou

_____

_____

_____

47

gomabseubnida! (Thank You! in Korean) –
in 140 languages http://aha.pub/thankyou

_____

_____

_____

48

Spas dikim! (Thank You! in Kurdish) –
in 140 languages http://aha.pub/thankyou

_____

_____

_____

49

Рахмат сага! (Thank You! in Kyrgyz) – in 140 languages http://aha.pub/thankyou

_____

_____

_____

50

ຂອບໃຈ! (Thank You! in Lao) –
in 140 languages http://aha.pub/thankyou

_____

_____

_____

51

Gratias tibi! (Thank You! in Latin) –
in 140 languages http://aha.pub/thankyou

_____

_____

_____

52

Paldies! (Thank You! in Latvian) –
in 140 languages http://aha.pub/thankyou

_____

_____

_____

53

Ačiū! (Thank You! in Lithuanian) –
in 140 languages http://aha.pub/thankyou

_____

_____

_____

54

Merci! (Thank You! in Luxembourgish) –
in 140 languages http://aha.pub/thankyou

_____

_____

_____

55

Ти благодарам! (Thank You! in Macedonian) – in 140 languages
http://aha.pub/thankyou

_____

_____

_____

56

Misaotra anao! (Thank You! in Malagasy) – in 140 languages http://aha.pub/thankyou

_____

_____

_____

57

Terima kasih! (Thank You! in Malay) –
in 140 languages http://aha.pub/thankyou

_____

_____

_____

58

നന്ദി! (Thank You! in Malayalam) –
in 140 languages http://aha.pub/thankyou

_____

_____

_____

59

Grazzi! (Thank You! in Maltese) –
in 140 languages http://aha.pub/thankyou

_____

_____

_____

60

Mauruuru koe! (Thank You! in Maori) –
in 140 languages http://aha.pub/thankyou

_____

_____

_____

61

धन्यवाद! (Thank You! in Marathi) –
in 140 languages http://aha.pub/thankyou

_____

_____

_____

62

та бүхэнд баярлалаа! (Thank You!
in Mongolian) – in 140 languages
http://aha.pub/thankyou

_____

_____

_____

63

धन्यवाद! (Thank You! in Nepali) –
in 140 languages http://aha.pub/thankyou

_____

_____

_____

64

Takk skal du ha! (Thank You! in Norwegian)
– in 140 languages http://aha.pub/thankyou

_____

_____

_____

65

Zikomo! (Thank You! in Nyanja) –
in 140 languages http://aha.pub/thankyou

_____

_____

_____

66

Dziękuję Ci! (Thank You! in Polish) –
in 140 languages http://aha.pub/thankyou

_____

_____

_____

67

Obrigado! (Thank You! in Portuguese) –
in 140 languages http://aha.pub/thankyou

_____

_____

_____

68

ਤੁਹਾਡਾ ਧੰਨਵਾਦ! (Thank You! in Punjabi) – in 140 languages http://aha.pub/thankyou

_____

_____

_____

69

Mulțumesc! (Thank You! in Romanian) – in 140 languages http://aha.pub/thankyou

_____

_____

_____

70

спасибо! (Thank You! in Russian) -
in 140 languages http://aha.pub/thankyou

71

faafetai! (Thank You! in Samoan) -
in 140 languages http://aha.pub/thankyou

72

Tapadh leat! (Thank You! in Scottish Gaelic)
– in 140 languages http://aha.pub/thankyou

_____

_____

_____

73

Хвала вам! (Thank You! in Serbian) –
in 140 languages http://aha.pub/thankyou

_____

_____

_____

74

Ndatenda! (Thank You! in Shona) –
in 140 languages http://aha.pub/thankyou

_____

_____

_____

75

ඔබට ස්තුතියි! (Thank You! in Sinhala) –
in 140 languages http://aha.pub/thankyou

_____

_____

_____

76

Ďakujem! (Thank You! in Slovak) –
in 140 languages http://aha.pub/thankyou

_____

_____

_____

77

Hvala! (Thank You! in Slovenian) –
in 140 languages http://aha.pub/thankyou

_____

_____

_____

78

Mahadsanid! (Thank You! in Somali) –
in 140 languages http://aha.pub/thankyou

_____

_____

_____

79

Gracias! (Thank You! in Spanish) –
in 140 languages http://aha.pub/thankyou

_____

_____

_____

80

hatur nuhun! (Thank You! in Sundanese) –
in 140 languages http://aha.pub/thankyou

_____

_____

_____

81

Asante! (Thank You! in Swahili) –
in 140 languages http://aha.pub/thankyou

_____

_____

_____

82

Tack! (Thank You! in Swedish) –
in 140 languages http://aha.pub/thankyou

_____

_____

_____

83

сипос! (Thank You! in Tajik) –
in 140 languages http://aha.pub/thankyou

_____

_____

_____

84

நன்றி! (Thank You! in Tamil) –
in 140 languages http://aha.pub/thankyou

_____

_____

_____

85

ధన్యయవ రాదరాలౖ! (Thank You! in Telugu) –
in 140 languages http://aha.pub/thankyou

_____

_____

_____

86

ขอขอบคุณ! (Thank You! in Thai) –
in 140 languages http://aha.pub/thankyou

_____

_____

_____

87

Teşekkür ederim! (Thank You! in Telugu) –
in 140 languages http://aha.pub/thankyou

_____

_____

_____

88

Дякую! (Thank You! in Ukrainian) –
in 140 languages http://aha.pub/thankyou

_____

_____

_____

89

rahmat! (Thank You! in Uzbek) –
in 140 languages http://aha.pub/thankyou

_____

_____

_____

90

Cảm ơn bạn! (Thank You! in Vietnamese) –
in 140 languages http://aha.pub/thankyou

_____

_____

_____

91

Diolch! (Thank You! in Welsh) –
in 140 languages http://aha.pub/thankyou

_____

_____

_____

92

Dankewol! (Thank You! in Western Frisian)
– in 140 languages http://aha.pub/thankyou

_____

_____

_____

93

Enkosi! (Thank You! in Xhosa) –
in 140 languages http://aha.pub/thankyou

_____

_____

_____

94

e dupe! (Thank You! in Yoruba) –
in 140 languages http://aha.pub/thankyou

_____

_____

_____

95

Ngiyabonga! (Thank You! in Zulu) –
in 140 languages http://aha.pub/thankyou

_____

_____

_____

96

ua tsaug! (Thank You! in Hmong Daw) –
in 140 languages http://aha.pub/thankyou

_____

_____

_____

97

Asante! (Thank You! in Kiswahili) – in 140 languages http://aha.pub/thankyou

_____

_____

_____

98

nuqneH! (Thank You! in Klingon) – in 140 languages http://aha.pub/thankyou

_____

_____

_____

99

Di jamädi! (Thank You!
in Queretaro Otomi) – in 140 languages
http://aha.pub/thankyou

_____

_____

_____

100

Nib óolal! (Thank You! in Yucatec Maya) –
in 140 languages http://aha.pub/thankyou

_____

_____

_____

101

Wiliwni! (Thank You! in Abenaki) –
in 140 languages http://aha.pub/thankyou

_____

_____

_____

102

Тхьауегъэпсэу! (Thank You! in Adyghe) –
in 140 languages http://aha.pub/thankyou

_____

_____

_____

103

Hioy'oy! (Thank You! in Ainu) –
in 140 languages http://aha.pub/thankyou

_____

_____

_____

104

Qaĝaasakung! (Thank You! in Aleut) –
in 140 languages http://aha.pub/thankyou

_____

_____

_____

105

Vielmohls mersi! (Thank You! in Alsatian) –
in 140 languages http://aha.pub/thankyou

_____

_____

_____

106

Grazias! (Thank You! in Aragonese) –
in 140 languages http://aha.pub/thankyou

_____

_____

_____

107

Tawdi sagi! (Thank You! in Aramaic) –
in 140 languages http://aha.pub/thankyou

_____

_____

_____

108

Hohóu! (Thank You! in Arapaho) –
in 140 languages http://aha.pub/thankyou

_____

_____

_____

109

Hristo multu! (Thank You! in Aromanian) –
in 140 languages http://aha.pub/thankyou

_____

_____

_____

110

Mikwetc! (Thank You! in Atikamekw) –
in 140 languages http://aha.pub/thankyou

_____

_____

_____

111

Mauliate! (Thank You! in Batak) –
in 140 languages http://aha.pub/thankyou

_____

_____

_____

112

Tsikomo! (Thank You! in Bemba) -
in 140 languages http://aha.pub/thankyou

_____

_____

_____

113

Tangkiu! (Thank You! in Bislama) -
in 140 languages http://aha.pub/thankyou

_____

_____

_____

114

Zikomo! (Thank You! in Chichewa) –
in 140 languages http://aha.pub/thankyou

_____

_____

_____

115

Tákk! (Thank You! in Elfdalian) –
in 140 languages http://aha.pub/thankyou

116

Akpe! (Thank You! in Ewe) –
in 140 languages http://aha.pub/thankyou

117

Graciis! (Thank You! in Friulian) –
in 140 languages http://aha.pub/thankyou

_____

_____

_____

118

Mitela! (Thank You! in Garo) –
in 140 languages http://aha.pub/thankyou

_____

_____

_____

119

Mèrcie bein des fais! (Thank You!
in Jèrriais) – in 140 languages
http://aha.pub/thankyou

_____

_____

_____

120

Khublei! (Thank You! in Khasi) –
in 140 languages http://aha.pub/thankyou

_____

_____

_____

121

Sepk'eec'a! (Thank You! in Klamath) –
in 140 languages http://aha.pub/thankyou

_____

_____

_____

122

Pilámaya! (Thank You! in Lakota Sioux) –
in 140 languages http://aha.pub/thankyou

_____

_____

_____

123

Merci! (Thank You! in Lingala) –
in 140 languages http://aha.pub/thankyou

_____

_____

_____

124

ki'ecai! (Thank You! in Lojban) –
in 140 languages http://aha.pub/thankyou

_____

_____

_____

125

Weebale! (Thank You! in Luganda) –
in 140 languages http://aha.pub/thankyou

_____

_____

_____

126

Gijtto! (Thank You! in Lule Sámi) –
in 140 languages http://aha.pub/thankyou

_____

_____

_____

127

Chjontexix! (Thank You! in Mam) –
in 140 languages http://aha.pub/thankyou

_____

_____

_____

128

Marci! (Thank You! in Michif) –
in 140 languages http://aha.pub/thankyou

_____

_____

_____

129

Ngiyabonga! (Thank You!
in Northern Ndebele) – in 140 languages
http://aha.pub/thankyou

_____

_____

_____

130

Ngiyathokoza! (Thank You!
in Southern Ndebele) – in 140 languages
http://aha.pub/thankyou

_____

_____

_____

131

Fakaaue (Thank You! in Niuean) –
in 140 languages http://aha.pub/thankyou

_____

_____

_____

132

Mercés! (Thank You! in Occitan) –
in 140 languages http://aha.pub/thankyou

_____

_____

_____

133

Nifee deebiru! (Thank You! in Okinawan) –
in 140 languages http://aha.pub/thankyou

_____

_____

_____

134

Merchi! (Thank You! in Picard) –
in 140 languages http://aha.pub/thankyou

_____

_____

_____

135

Tanggio! (Thank You! in Pijin) –
in 140 languages http://aha.pub/thankyou

_____

_____

_____

136

Hantanye! (Thank You! in Quenya) –
in 140 languages http://aha.pub/thankyou

_____

_____

_____

137

Maururu! (Thank You! in Rapanui) –
in 140 languages http://aha.pub/thankyou

_____

_____

_____

138

Noa'ia! (Thank You! in Rotuman) –
in 140 languages http://aha.pub/thankyou

_____

_____

_____

139

Fa'afetai tele! (Thank You! in Samoan) –
in 140 languages http://aha.pub/thankyou

_____

_____

_____

140

Ke a leboga! (Thank You! in Setswana) –
in 140 languages http://aha.pub/thankyou

_____

_____

_____

About the Author

Mitchell Levy @HappyAbout is the CEO and Thought Leader Architect at THiNKaha and The AHA Guy at AHAthat. He and his team make it easy for corporations to create compelling content that helps turn their experts into recognized thought leaders.

AHAthat makes it easy to share, author, and promote content. There are over 37,000 quotes (AHAmessages™) by thought leaders from around the world that you can share in seconds for free.

For those who want to author their own book, we have time-tested proven processes that allow you to write your AHAbook™ of 140 digestible, bite-sized morsels in eight hours or less. Once your content is on AHAthat, you have a customized link that you can use to have your fans/advocates share your content and help grow your network.

⟳ Start sharing: http://AHAthat.com

⟳ Start authoring: http://AHAthat.com/Author

Please go directly to this book in AHAthat and share each AHAmessage socially at http://aha.pub/ThankYou.

Own a Phrase,
Make It Your Own!

Is there a phrase that you're known for or want to be known for? Want us to create a social media-enabled eBook and physical book for you with that phrase in 100+ languages?

Check out http://aha.pub/Phrases for our growing library of phrase books.

Want More Info? Contact THiNKaha (CustomBooks@thinkaha.com, 408-257-3000).